HOW TO DO A GEMBA WALK

Walk with a Purpose

MICHAEL BREMER

The Cumberland Group

Cover design: Laura Shinn – laurashinn.author@gmail.com
E-book/print book formatting: Sue Trowbridge – interbridge.com
Copy editing: Diane Piron-Gelman – wordnrd@earthlink.net

Note: We did an amendment to the book in January, 2016. We added a section on doing a Gemba Walk in an office or administrative environment and we expanded the section on coaching Gemba walkers.

CONTENTS

GEMBA WALK DEFINITION

GEMBA WALKS

Many books have been written about performance improvement using some form of Lean (which is based on the Toyota Production System) or Six Sigma, which originated at Motorola and was popularized by General Electric. If you did an analysis of improvement effectiveness you would find that most organizations do get better after adopting an improvement methodology, but they typically fail to radically transform their competitive position or to significantly alter the way the organization engages its employees.

We have spent time studying a number of organizations including: Autoliv (Americas), OC Tanner, Cogent Power and Menlo Innovations. Each of these companies followed a slightly different pathway toward becoming highly effective at improving. We have also gained insights via the Manufacturing Excellence Award recipients from the Association of Manufacturing Excellence.

In this guide we focus on one powerful element of their improvement activities: Gemba Walks. Even if you currently do Gemba Walks, in all likelihood you fall short of what the best companies do. Gemba Walks help leaders to distinguish between process and people. When you look at processes with a 'Capital P' your first question is always, "Why was the process not capable of handling this situation?"

- If a new employee fails at a task. Is there a problem with the on-boarding process or the training process?

- If a hospital administers an incorrect medication. Is there a problem with equipment calibration processes, communication processes between physician, nurse and/or pharmacy, the way medications are labeled, etc.?

- In an office environment where work is delivered incorrectly or delivered late. Is there a problem with the way workload gets managed, with requirement definition processes, with the way the organization measures performance, with how capacity is managed, etc.?

It's easiest to assign blame and then move-on. A deeper and better fix is to address the underlying process issues.

Every organization has performance problems, but taking a "process view first" changes the way we look at those problems. Toyota holds people to a high standard of accountability, but it's always filtered through process-tinted glasses, so that the organization first of all takes responsibility for all performance problems; Toyota leaders do not blame the person. This creates a much more open environment for problem visibility.

Early in the journey no matter what words get expressed, people feel they will be blamed when a problem arises. Leaders going to Gemba can use this knowledge to help people understand it's not about "who to blame." Instead, walkers focus on trying to gain a better understanding of process performance. They separate process and people. Once people begin to believe leaders truly do separate these two dimensions, people become more comfortable sharing real issues and concerns.

There is a desperate need around the world for better leadership. While this book is not primarily focused on leadership, you can use the principles discussed to become a more effective leader. *I hope you do.*

Gemba Walk Definition

A Gemba Walk is an alternate expression for the Japanese term "Genchi Genbutsu," which on a Toyota website is defined as, "Going to the source to find the facts to make correct decisions, build consensus, and achieve goals." A common slang expression for this is "Get your boots on and go see the reality." In other words, don't make dangerous assumptions about things you only know from a distance.

Gemba Walks represent a potential learning and development opportunity both for the walkers and the people being visited during the walk. The amount of learning and discovery that takes place largely depends on how effectively the walk gets done, thus the reason for writing this guide. An ineffective walk will actually hinder an organization's improvement ability. An effective walk can increase credibility and build trust for all involved parties.

A Gemba Walk is part of the "Study and Adjust" steps in the Plan/Do/Study/Adjust problem-solving methodology. When you walk the Gemba (where the action is inside your organization), you have an opportunity to "See or to Study" with your own eyes and more deeply understand *what is really happening* inside your organization. That's in contrast to what we might assume is happening in areas where others do the real value-adding day-to-day work, and the rest of us provide support in indirect ways (e.g., supervising, planning workloads, scheduling, coordinating materials logistics, coordinating lab tests, patient transportation, coordinating with other departments/functional groups, etc.) as different customer orders, requests, products, patients, etc. flow through our value-adding process activities. You also have an opportunity to discover which processes inside your business need adjustment, as they inhibit people's ability to do the right thing.

Seek Understanding

The model for doing a Gemba Walk is actually quite simple.

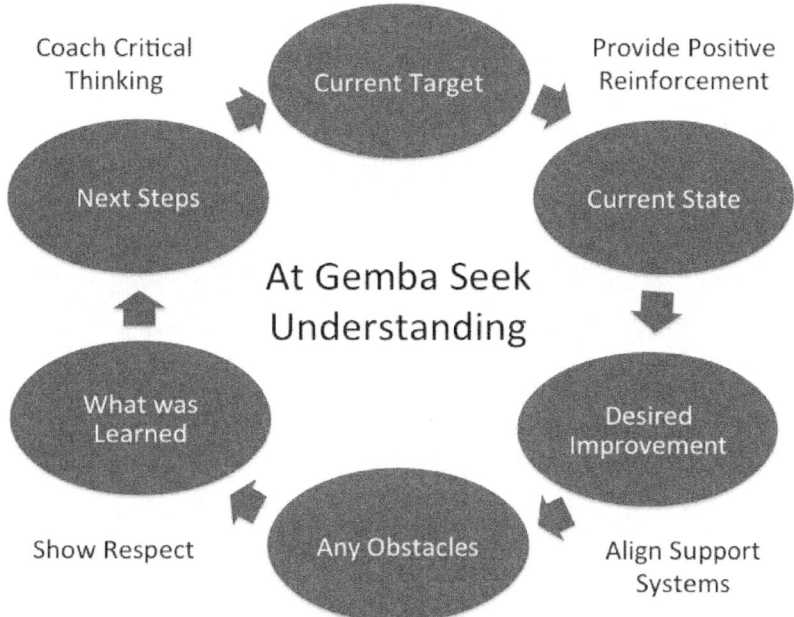

The walkers seek to better understand:

1. The current and future state targets for the area being observed (what is it, why is that the target?).

2. The current state (what is the current reality, the current condition) of the process(es) observed.

3. What improvement is being worked and why? Is this being done in a scientific fashion following some type of Plan/Do/Study/Adjust methodology?

4. Are any obstacles hindering progress? Is there something the walkers can do to alleviate them?

5. What was learned from the improvement experiments?

6. What are the next steps?

The walkers support changing the culture of the organization when they:

1. **Coach** people to develop their critical thinking skills executing the above model

2. Provide **positive reinforcement** supporting the experiments and the learning taking place

3. Seek to **better align** management support systems to streamline cross-functional performance.

4. **Show respect** to everyone, at every level participating in the Gemba Walk process

The rest of this book breaks the above process into three general steps: Go See; Ask What, Then Why; and Show Respect. This model is reinforced in Mike Rother's book Toyota Kata, which is briefly described later in this volume.

According to John Shook[1], *"Go see, ask why, show respect'* is the way we turn the philosophy of scientific empiricism into actual behavior." It's an expression he originally learned from Fujio Cho (past president and chairman of Toyota). In an LEI blog, Shook went on to say, "We go observe what is really happening (at the Gemba where the work takes place), while showing respect for the people involved, especially the people who do the real value-creating work of the business."

VALUE

Going to the Gemba where "value" is actually created or

1. http://www.lean.org/shook/displayobject.cfm?o=1843

delivered to customers is a powerful learning experience for anyone whose job provides support to the value creators.

The most simplistic definition (formula) of Value Added for a manufacturing company is Sales Price – Materials Costs = Value Added. In industrial engineering the term "Value Added" is defined as something that changes the form, the fit or the function of a product. We have always looked at Value Added from a slightly different perspective.

A very select group of people literally creates value for an organization. It includes the people who design the product or service, the people who make the product or deliver the service, and to some degree the people who talk to customers about the product or service (typically sales and customer service). These are all direct "customer facing" responsibilities. Everyone else in the organization should be supporting the people who create value. You need to be very clear in understanding the value-creating responsibilities in your organization. In some organizations, a supporting department (finance, scheduling, HR, information systems, etc.) can emerge as the dominant group and this can cause dysfunctional behavior by arbitrarily focusing attention and resources on non-value-adding functions, which may actually inhibit the company's ability to deliver value at a competitive price.

EFFECTIVE LEADERSHIP

Jack Zenger and Joseph Folkman wrote an article for the *Harvard Business Review* in June, 2009 titled,"Ten Fatal Flaws That Derail Leaders". Gemba Walks can have a strong positive impact on each of the items they list in the article, especially their key point regarding how *leaders fail to develop others; they focus on themselves to the exclusion of developing subordinates,* causing individuals and teams to disengage.

Gemba Walks provide an opportunity to address the issues described in the Zenger/Folkman article. All *effective leaders* do the following Steps 1 and 2. Those same two steps have become the primary purpose of most Gemba Walks. According to Dr. Jeffrey Liker, "Doing a Gemba Walk has become a common lean practice and people assume, 'it's simply going to the Gemba to understand the work, be present, and see the issues' — in other words, sort of a random walk to find problems."

1. Set direction with challenging targets

2. Learn to more effectively see problems, abnormalities, waste, and opportunities

Great leaders, including the companies in our study, move beyond the leadership basics and incorporate Steps 3, 4, and 5. The latter three steps increase trust levels with employees and between cross-functional work groups. They also serve as powerful change levers if incorporated into your Gemba Walks.

3. Teach/coach associates to develop their ability to perform and to fix and improve their processes

4. Have the tenacity to stay the course, yet balance that drive with a humility that permits them stay in touch with reality as it actually exists

5. Align support systems to elevate the organization's improvement maturity

A respectful, effective Gemba Walk builds trust and lays the groundwork for a major transformation! It is amazing what one can learn during a walk! *How can you be an effective leader and not want to do this?*

GET IN TOUCH WITH REALITY

We are about to say something many people probably know is true, but still find very difficult to believe. Most leadership teams' assumptions about what is happening in the workplace on a day-to-day basis do not align with the reality of what is actually taking place. Does that sound surprising to you? We hope not, as much has been written about this subject, so we don't wish to belabor it. But we can pretty much guarantee if you follow the guidelines suggested in this e-book, you will be surprised at what you learn.

A senior executive from a Fortune 30 firm recently shared this story. *"We were doing a Gemba Walk and discovered that one work station was about to miss takt time. When we asked why, we were told an operator had to grind a coupler, which was not part of standard work. We asked why and they said it didn't fit in the coupler pocket. We asked why a second time and nobody knew the answer. So we asked them to check the drawing dimensions and we would discuss in the next Walk. We were back 4 hours later and asked what they found. They said, 'The part was to spec but they were actually grinding it out of spec.' We asked, if the part was to spec, then why would they grind it out of spec? They said, 'to make it fit!'*

"We suggested if it was to spec and did not fit, then there must be an issue with the coupler pocket dimension. We asked them to get the drawing and check the dimensions and we would follow up on the next walk. The next walk was late in the day and they said, 'the coupler pocket was to spec.' It made no sense. We then checked the drawing dates and realized they had not been revised in 40 years. There was a stack-up tolerance issue, and for 40 years teams had been grinding couplers, when needed, out of spec to fit and missing takt each time they did it. Possibly 40 years earlier an operator could not get the parts to fit and a foreman told him to grind it and make it fit.

"For more than 40 years no one ever asked 'Why?' and people continued to work that way. A practice that unfortunately is quite normal in most companies. This is just one example! It is definitely worthwhile to Go See as it provides an opportunity to create an environment where more people ask, 'Why?'"

Gemba Walks offer a way for the walkers to change their perspective in how they see, understand and manage their organization. Gemba Walks are about helping everyone in the organization to more clearly see and understand the *whole process* as a first step in identifying ways to improve it. True industry leaders are using Gemba Walk methods to empower the entire workforce for continuous operational improvement. Lesser competitors cannot keep pace with that.

WHY DO A GEMBA WALK?

If getting in touch with reality and changing your perspective isn't sufficient, what other reasons exist to do a Gemba Walk? Consider three keys: Purpose, Process and People.

We have already touched upon the *first key reason*: **Purpose**. Gemba Walks provide a wonderful opportunity to learn if people inside the organization have a deep understanding of why they are doing their work activities and why this work is necessary. Every job in the organization should have some importance, some reason for existence. The same is true for departments. People often get caught up in the activities they do without developing a deeper understanding of why those actions are important.

If people understand the purpose, the underlying reason why their work is necessary, they are in a much better position to find improvement opportunities. Developing more critical thinking skills should ultimately be the key purpose of any Gemba Walk. *Lean transformations only happen if the people transform.* The walker seeks to learn:

1. Depth of understanding people have about the work they do

2. How people approach trying to make improvement happen, current mental models used inside the organization

3. Actions needed by leadership to take the organization's improvement maturity to a higher level

4. Compliance to standard work

5. Progress toward current short-, medium- and long-term goals of the processes

6. Problems/abnormalities present in the current condition, as well as activities underway to resolve them

7. Opportunities and improvement ideas and plans that are underway

The *second key reason* deals with **Process**. Are work activities effectively aligned between departments and between work groups with what the organization is trying to accomplish? It is critical to get an understanding of process performance, as this is the source of most performance issues. Since customers are served as a result of different functional groups working together, it is important to maximize performance across the various functions or across the overall value stream, not to maximize performance for individual component pieces (silos).

In his book *Out of the Crisis*, Dr. W. Edwards Deming said, "Management by walking around is hardly ever effective." The reason being that someone in management, walking around, typically has little idea about what questions to ask, and usually does not pause long enough at any spot to get the right answer. Dr. Deming also stated quite clearly, "Most problems

(*85% to 95%*) are system (*process*) problems, not people problems." Gemba Walks provide a structured approach for assessing process performance and bringing key issues to the surface. Just asking about performance metrics during a walk and how those metrics affect upstream or downstream work groups can yield meaningful insights that call for support system adjustments.

The *third key reason* for doing these walks, and perhaps the most important, is to develop ***People.*** A walk is an opportunity for leaders to learn how to create a more effective environment where:

1. People can do their best work
2. People can fully develop their skills and capabilities
3. Trust levels can increase
4. People feel safe in sharing problems experienced in their work

A Toyota Japanese trainer once made the statement, "When you go to the floor for a problem, go with two brains. One to understand the problem that needs to be worked and how to teach the members to solve it, and one to see all of the 'system' problems that are occurring, which are 'your problems' to work on."

As a leader, it is not your job to identify or fix the local problem. If you take responsibility for the fix, you will have a lot of extra work to do and you remove ownership from the people in the work environment. Remember, it's important to get team members to "play back" coaching or guidance they receive as the walk is being done, to make certain team members truly understand. Although we are unsure of the true source for this quote, it is a good thought: "If the student hasn't learned, the teacher hasn't taught."

Mike Hoseus, former Assistant General Manager at Toyota Motor Engineering and Manufacturing, said, *"For us, the Gemba Walk was a way to live out the 'Servant Leadership' principle we were taught. A big part of our focus was building a relationship of mutual trust and respect on our walks."*

If you understand the process and you understand how people who operate within the process think and act about performing Standard Work and capturing improvement opportunities, then you are well on your way to understanding the fundamental problems facing your organization.

Many organizations get stuck at an average level of performance because they promote the wrong people and do not have a holistic understanding of process performance. These types of organizations typically recognize and promote leaders in organizational silos who seemingly accomplish their mission within the organization by hitting their numbers or performance targets. But they do not take time to develop a deeper understanding of what is really happening from a process perspective. The organization then suffers major setbacks as a result of poor decision-making by people who looked like they were doing a good job, but their replacements are left with a work group, team, department or division that is unable to perform moving forward. It is not easy to see the longer-term ramifications of short-term decision-making. Gemba Walkers can more clearly see what is really happening.

Gemba Walkers can also identify outstanding new talent,

something especially important during times of transition and competitive challenge. The walks reveal more about the character and capability of potential future leaders and help to pierce this cloak of invisibility. The walker can identify people with outstanding leadership potential, those capable of developing and engaging employees, working effectively with their peers and accomplishing their mission. It's a much more holistic view of an effective leader.

Having gained these insights, the walkers can better align organizational support systems and further develop employee skills to solve problems. Effective Gemba Walkers coach team members how to see the world this way. Organizations highly effective at improving develop people's critical thinking skills, build a high degree of trust between associates and leaders, and foster an environment of accountability where people are passionately involved in improvement.

CREATE AN ENVIRONMENT OF EXPERIMENTATION AND LEARNING

Every Gemba Walk is a teaching exercise. The way questions do/do not get asked has a big impact on people. People at the worksite are also observing. Thoughts are constantly going through their heads: "What does the leader want to know? If I share something that's wrong, what will happen? Does this person really want to know what is happening? Is it worth taking a risk and saying what I truly believe?" So the way the walk gets done is always important.

Leaders in companies that are highly effective at improving all seem to have one common trait in the way they behave. They lead with a high degree of humility and a willingness to learn. As these leaders grew from leading organizations that were good at improving to a much higher level of improvement maturity, they radically changed their perspective regarding how to improve.

One way to help create this environment is to focus on performance targets, with a process mindset that takes into account the suppliers and customers for the work being done. Organizations usually have overall future performance targets, but they are often missing a future state performance target at the department or work-team level. There should be two target conditions (goals) people strive to hit in the work they do. People usually focus on the first one and often miss the second:

1. What is the current performance target?
2. What is the "future state" performance target?

Appropriate questions to ask might be:

1. Are the targets clear, and how effectively are they being addressed?
2. Who are the customers for this process and how do you know they are well served?
3. What has been learned from actions taken?
4. What are the next actions planned?

The Gemba Walk can be used to encourage people to create an environment of experimentation and learning focused on reaching a desired future state level of accomplishment.

Mike Rother has done quite a bit of research on how Toyota learns and does problem solving. A key part of it is an effective coaching process. It's a variation on some of the other dialogues outlined in his book and in fact it could be the model you use for your Gemba Walk discussions. In *Toyota Kata*, which describes patterns of thought and action inside Toyota, he provides a methodology for operating with these dual targets.

You can apply Kata-type language in your conversations about how to improve your Gemba Walks. Rother's model, outlined below, is based on a five-step iteration of learning and improving to coach people using five basic questions:

1. What is the target condition (Understand the direction)?
2. What is the actual current condition (Grasp the current condition)?

    A. What was your last step (the step you took trying to improve)?

    B. What did you expect (to happen)?

    C. What actually happened?

    D. What did you learn (from the experiment)?

3. What obstacles do you think are preventing you from reaching the target condition?
4. What is your next step (Plan/Do/Check/Act problem-solving experiment)? What do you expect to see as a result of that experiment?
5. How can we Go See what we have learned from taking that step?

Once the target condition is realized and stable, then establish the next target condition. Begin the next cycle of continuous improvement.

Process Name:		Challenge:	
Target Condition:	Current Condition:	PDCA Cycles Record	
		Obstacles Parking Lot	
© M Rother - Improvement Kata Workbook (used with permission)			

The model is explained in much more detail in *Toyota Kata*. Additional information, including a number of problem-solving forms and analytical guides, is available on their website: http://www-personal.umich.edu/~mrother/ Handbook/Appendix.pdf

STANDARD WORK AND GEMBA WALKS

A primary reason improvements are difficult to sustain is the typical instability of business processes. Processes are rife with exceptions, workarounds get done on a daily basis to resolve problems, and effective "standard work" practices are often lacking.

In most organizations, Standard Work is misunderstood and vastly under-utilized. Standard Work should be the best-known practice for doing work. It applies to highly repetitive work in manufacturing, in transaction environments like call centers and claims processing, as well as transporting patients within a health care provider's facility.

Standard Work also applies to other types of activities: a supervisor checking the status of performance, an executive coming into a facility to review operations, a team or management review meeting, doing the accounting close, etc.

Essentially, Standard Work should be the best-known way to get work accomplished. It also typically incorporates the pace at which work should happen, when it should occur, and a desire to make it easier to see (make it visual) if the right thing is being done at the right time.

If an organization does not have reasonably effective

Standard Work practices, then doing Gemba Walks poses a challenge. Why? Because so much variation exists in the way work gets done that it's difficult to do a reliable observation.

Consider two simple examples to better understand the above concept. The actual situation in both examples was more complex, but the essence of the points made below reflects the reality of the situations.

Example 1: A foundation that funds research in the healthcare sector decides to improve its grant request process. However, different program managers at the foundation require varying amounts of information. One program manager likes to see a detailed budget; another program manager likes to look at high-level numbers only. When applicants submit their requests for funding, some applications are received incomplete, but because the foundation wants to get an early start on processing the request, managers begin to work on it. If the foundation were to implement improvements to the grant request process (e.g., moving from paper to web-based applications) with this amount of variation being permitted throughout the process, there would be no simple way to measure the impact of that change.

Example 2: A manufacturing company seeks to improve a changeover process in one of its manufacturing cells. The team does a great job of analyzing internal and external times and implements a series of improvements. Yet the cell suffers from insufficiently available materials, or there are quality problems (variation) with the materials, or the people responsible for programming the machine are not always available when it's time to do the changeover, etc.

In each of these examples, changes (improvements) might get

made to the above processes, but because the processes themselves are so unstable, it is difficult to know exactly what impact an improvement might have had, and it is challenging to sustain any new methods due to the variations. People working in both these organizations would do a workaround when problems occurred, trying to do the right thing, but unintentionally hiding the causes of process instability as a result. *The Gemba Walker's goal is to begin to "see" the discrepancy between the way we want to do work vs. the way work is actually getting done.*

The repetitive focus of Gemba Walks and more use of Standard Work typically leads to breakthrough achievements and increases your level of employee engagement. Sometimes people worry about Standard Work practices stifling creativity. In reality, defining a best practice as "Standard Work" and then doing Gemba Walks to see how effectively it is operating allows creativity to emerge that results in even more effective work practices. This idea is not new. Many years ago Aristotle said, "Through discipline, comes freedom."

Once an organization begins to stabilize its processes, an amazing thing happens! More time becomes available to concentrate on the longer-term, strategic issues that will move the organization forward, because people have to deal with fewer exceptions and fewer variations from the norm (Standard Work).

As Mike Rother puts it in *Toyota Kata*: *"Perhaps the most important thing for a leader to focus on during a Gemba Walk is not the content of what people are working on, but the pattern of thinking and acting they utilize as they improve and strive for goals."* If you can improve the critical thinking skills of your workforce and help the organization become better and faster at implementing improvements, a Gemba Walk may be one of the most productive uses of your time. The walks provide an opportunity to uncover hidden abnormalities taking place on a day-to-day basis.

With the philosophy behind Gemba Walks now in mind, we can move on to the mechanics of doing them. Like all collaborative performances, the overall plan and details are important.

STEP-BY-STEP GEMBA WALK

A consistent step-by-step structure and standard work for Gemba Walks is especially important in the learning phase. None of the steps involved is "rocket science," but Gemba Walks are complex with many component parts. Typically, a walk requires developing new habits and often requires a behavior shift for many managers.

The following outline provides an overview of the most common features of Gemba Walks. You might also wish to check the specific Gemba Walk Example Guides to see if one of them better fits your immediate needs. Eventually you should build your own, customized standard work outline designed for your specific situation.

A simple structural model is needed to keep it all in context. Three stages that should be done for any Gemba Walk include:

Three Stages – Gemba Walk

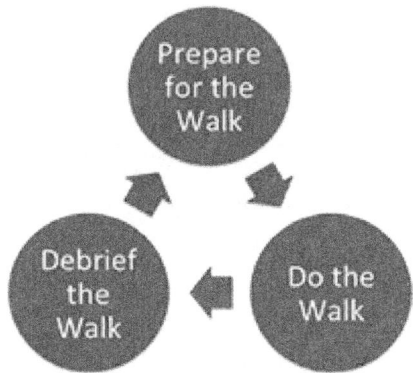

1. Preparation Prior to the Walk

2. Doing the Walk

3. Debrief Activities After the Walk

You will become more effective in your Gemba Walks with practice. You learn by doing. Going to *see the real work* first-hand, and *asking what and then why* are practiced throughout the typical Gemba Walk steps. Always *show respect* to the people you interact with during all phases of the walk.

Coaching of the walkers is beneficial for improving your effectiveness. After many practice runs, a walk becomes more routine and dependable. Post-walk follow-up actions include making certain the gains are sustained and coaching the Gemba Walkers to become more effective at doing the walk.

Throughout this guide we discuss the types of questions that are appropriate to ask as you walk the Gemba. **Asking the appropriate question is one of a walker's most important**

responsibilities. Becoming good at Gemba Walks can transform a person from a good leader to a great leader. It is worth the effort!

PREPARATION PRIOR TO THE WALK

An effective walk builds trust and understanding. It fosters the development of a *shared* vision where people working together can accomplish performance improvements to make the organization more successful. When people co-own a "vision," it is much stronger than nice words on the wall. Creating this type of environment should be the core purpose of any walk. *It must be done in a no-blame environment.* Otherwise people will simply tell the leader what they think he or she wants to hear and they will sugarcoat any problems. *The leader should always look to the process as the source of errors, never at the people.* Said a different way, leaders should always jump to the "5 whys," never the "5 whos."

With this in mind, here are a few basic steps that should be done before heading out to Gemba.

1. Define a Purpose for the Walk

Write down the purpose for your walk. It should be clear and meaningful. This is especially important when you first start doing walks, and should be shared/agreed-upon by the group doing the walk. The purpose statement can be used as part of coaching and debriefing activities. Typical purposes are:

A. Coach subordinates on process thinking, standard work and improvement

B. Get in touch with reality about how the business really works

C. Gain a deeper understanding of obstacles inhibiting service to customers

D. Search for improvement opportunities

Use the sample questions in this book as a guide, but it is important to create your own questions. Do the walkers truly understand what the customer(s) of the area/product/process/service being visited value, in terms of specs, time, cost, delivery, or other hard requirements? Getting good answers to these questions serves as a true north compass point and creates a frame of reference for the walkers to link all their observations and findings. So practice getting better at asking relevant questions. It will improve your walks.

2. Engage Associates in Advance

Show respect for associates in advance of any Gemba Walk by informing them of the walk's purpose, what the walkers need to see, and how the local team members might help the walkers to better understand how day-to-day work happens. Advance notification helps to avoid the possibility of the walk coming across as a "surprise party" that might cause associates alienation or embarrassment.

All associates in the work area should feel free to participate as empowered business team members and to offer information about the process, positive or negative, that might be useful to the walkers in ongoing CI activities.

Caution associates to avoid doing any pre-walk cleanup or metric/information board modifications in the area being walked. Those actions will undermine the usefulness of the walk.

3. Define a Scope for the Walk

Be clear about the area you want to walk. There is no one single starting point or itinerary for doing a walk. Where will you start and where will you finish? In a multi-shift operation, don't just do Gemba Walks on the day shift. Collaborate with the local process leadership to determine what should be included "in walk" to suit your purposes. Do you plan to:

A. Follow the flow to gain a better understanding of the process (e.g., pretend you are a piece of work and follow the process backwards from the end to the beginning).

B. Observe physical work cells and functional department areas in production plants, distribution centers, hospitals, service departments... perhaps looking at the tools, fixtures and storage devices used at each operation or standard work practices.

C. Observe information process flows through the screens and desk-tops of proposal preparation staffs, order processing teams, production and inventory planning teams, etc.

D. View the value stream covering the value-adding operations and key support functions of an entire product and/or services value stream.

E. Sometimes a walk requires you to observe real customer service interactions. At W.W. Grainger, walkers would stand at branch service counters and watch the associates interact with customers. Sometimes, they interviewed the customers after the service was complete to find out about their experience and value. To walk a service or non-physical process takes a little more thought, but is very doable. Those activities are subject to the same foibles, missteps and inconsistencies as any physical process.

F. Make certain you are prepared to check on progress with improvements agreed upon from prior Gemba Walks. (You will lose credibility if follow-up does not get done, and gain credibility if you handle it in a calm, thoughtful manner).

Determine who should join the walk based on the purpose and scope. Your walkers may be operations leaders from upstream or downstream departments, staff members from Quality, EH&S, Human Resources, Purchasing, Maintenance, Scheduling, Materials Control, Customer Service, etc. Do not invite walk participants who do not have a reason to be interested.

Depending on the location of the walk, walkers may need safety gear, clipboards, headsets, etc. Plan for this before the activity.

Standardize the cadence of the walk: Where to start, target time at each area. All areas may not be walked every day (the size of the transformation will dictate this).

4. Coach the Walk Participants Before Doing the Walk

Meet with the people doing the walk immediately prior to it.

Share the purpose and outline expectations for the walk (this can take less than 5 minutes and helps to clarify appropriate behaviors during the walk). This ensures a sharp focus on what should be achieved, and why. From the pre-walk communications, remind participants of the few key things they need to keep in mind during the walk:

A. Follow appropriate behavioral norms while the walk is being done. For example:

    a. Listen more than you talk

    b. Ask open-ended questions, to better understand your workers' processes (review Gemba Walk Questions from relevant examples in this booklet or from the list developed for your organization)

    c. Avoid asking questions that blame someone or some department for the problem. It may take some practice to get good at dropping "blame" from your questions.

    d. Make no on-the-spot judgments, positive or negative

    e. One conversation at a time, no sidebars, respect the person talking

    f. If multiple leaders go on the walk, ensure that one of them is assigned as the overall leader. Other leaders should let them lead, engaging only to clarify or add substance. Leaders should not debate, argue, or disagree with each other in front of associates… save the debate for later.

g. Behave respectfully to team members during the walk

h. Turn off your mobile devices to avoid interruptions

i. Remember to thank the SMEs for their expert explanations

B. During a waste walk, remind the walkers to keep their own notes on observed Strengths Done Well (+) and Opportunities for Improvement (–). These notes can be collected and clarified for feedback or used as part of the discussion in a subsequent walk as part of ongoing CI activities.

Refer to the section "Coaching the Gemba Walkers" for a few additional thoughts.

5. Coaching Tips for the Area Leader Before Hosting Gemba Walkers

In order to host a successful walk, do *not* do any extra pre-walk cleanup or metric/information board modifications in the area being walked. Such actions will defeat the purpose of the exercise. It is appropriate to:

A. **Prepare** – Let your team members know a Gemba Walk will take place. Encourage them to respond to questions and share their thinking. Ensure that people understand, if information is to be shared, it should be in the exact form and way they use it every day, not scrubbed clean to look nice.

B. **Make eye contact** – Speak loudly and clearly when

talking to/with the walkers (use a megaphone if needed to ensure all can hear, to encourage engagement).

C. **Face the audience** – When speaking, face the walkers, not an information board.

D. **Be inclusive** – Seek input from others.

E. **Share what YOU are doing** – Let the walkers know actions being performed by the team and let them know what help you need.

F. **Receive feedback** – As an area leader, be coachable, not defensive (Value Stream Coach should guide discussion when it gets off track).

G. **Collaborate** – Foster an environment of collaboration with the work team, team leads, supervisors, the walkers and other departments to develop solutions best for customers and the company overall.

The exact wording of questions will differ somewhat between a factory and a hospital, but in both environments the walker is trying to better understand the organization's value creation process. When you do the walk, you are seeking barriers and interruptions that inhibit people's ability to perform value-adding actions.

DOING THE WALK

This is the on-floor, main part of the Gemba Walk. All walkers should practice "active listening" and respectfully ask probing questions based on three key activities: *Go See, Ask What Then Why,*and *Show Respect*. These three behaviors are all part of **Doing the Walk**. Always show respect, because that sets the tone and expectations for whatever can or should happen next.

1. Go See

When you walk the Gemba, you realize some things you assume are happening are in fact not happening, and other things may be happening that you never anticipated. An open-minded walker can gain many new insights. For example, you may go to the floor to follow up on an injury and find out that the entire "new hire training" system is not being followed, or when you go to see and follow up on a defect you may learn that cross-training standards are not being followed.

A Gemba Walk lets you see first-hand if the people who work in your organization:

A. Understand the purpose of their work

B. Understand and follow Standard Work practices

C. Understand performance expectations

D. Use a scientific thought process for issue identification and root cause analysis

E. Create effective plans and actions to improve the processes toward the targets

F. Can sustain gains, or if processes beyond their control inhibit their ability to do effective work

G. Are inhibited, perhaps almost prohibited from doing the right thing due to silo mentalities in the various departments and work groups

Gemba walking starts with going to see, to gain a better understanding of the work being done.

2. Ask What, Then Why

When you ask "why" and have a *blame-free culture*, the truth comes out, along with all of the gaps. Doing a careful Gemba Walk with the process subject matter experts (SMEs) can be a tremendously enlightening activity for everyone involved. Seeing up close how a process actually works — vs. conditioned assumptions — can answer a host of questions that lead to new ideas for ways to develop people and major process improvements. A well-framed "humble question" helps to develop people's critical thinking skills. Questions should not be asked to prove people wrong; *the best questions help the person discover the answer herself.*

First questions should focus around "What?"

A. What is the primary purpose of this work activity (step)?

B. What are the main work steps in this job/cell/functional area?

C. What are you trying to accomplish?

D. What happens next after your work activity (step)?

At the process metrics board, ask:

A. How do you know if you are doing an effective job?

B. How do you measure a successful work day?

C. What is the target performance? Why is that the target?

D. Are we going to meet takt time this hour? If not, why not?

E. Who are the customers for the work you do? What are their requirements?

F. What product defects occur here?

G. What are the major abnormalities in this process?

H. What are typical problems or interruptions that occur in a workday? What happens when they occur?

Observe the overall process to gain an understanding, look for inconsistencies, and find things that are difficult to do:

A. Is the line/cell/group staffed with trained members per Standard Work?

B. Does the WIP amount equal the standard?

C. Is there material available for the team to obtain this takt or hour?

D. Is the material available for the next takt or hours, per plan?

E. Are operators capable of reaching planned cycle time per Standard Work?

F. Does the equipment enable stability? How can you judge?

G. Do people have to look around for things? Does time get wasted searching?

H. Are things where they are actually needed?

Observe the individual process steps. Learn what is happening so you can more effectively coach improvement actions. Take notice of actions or work activities that seem awkward or interrupt flow. Note where and how many times work (products, orders, patients, etc.) waits for approvals, or transportation, or the next work step:

A. What signals get sent to pull work (or patients) to the next level (look at upstream and downstream connections to other work groups)?

B. How do operators (professional staff) perceive upstream and downstream colleagues?

C. Do people wait for approval, inspections, results from other departments (e.g., test)?

After the walker has a basic understanding regarding the purpose of this work activity, "why"-type questions can be asked. It is appropriate to continue asking Why?' as issues arise to gain a deeper understanding of the possible root cause (5 Whys):

A. How do you know this is the right way to do your job?

B. Why is performance less than the desired target?

C. How do disruptions affect the workflow, cause wasted time?

D. Why do defects or process abnormalities occur?

E. Why does backtracking, rework, looking for things, occur?

F. Why is the line over/under-staffed?

G. Why is the WIP out of standard?

H. Why is there no material or too much material?

I. Why does work get done this way?

J. Why has this issue not been addressed?

For a first-time walker, you might approach your walk in this fashion. When approaching a work area, introduce yourself to a work team member. You might say, "Hi, I'm John Doe, vice president of Customer Service. May I ask a couple of questions about your work activities, work process (or operations, workflow, or…)?" Then make use of the questions outlined above as appropriate.

3. Show Respect

All walks should help the leader learn what is really happening and at the same time focus on helping people to maintain their dignity. This can only happen if the leaders create a safe place to have a conversation, and they show respect to the people they encounter along the way. Why would anyone openly discuss problems in their work area if he or she will be embarrassed once workplace issues are revealed, or if the walker looks as if he or she is trying to catch someone doing something wrong? Disrespecting people during a Gemba Walk provides no real value; it makes the leader look like a bully and causes people to hide problems. People will try to show their situation in the most positive light in order to stay out of trouble in this type of an environment.

Some leaders may have a deep understanding of the process they are observing. Given their work experience and knowledge, they might in fact have the best "right answer" to a particular problem and be in a position to provide it. However, when they act in that fashion, they are doing two things. First, they are telling the employee that they do not believe the employee is capable of finding the solution. Second, they are missing a big opportunity to help that individual with personal discovery, and deeper building of knowledge and capability. John Shook has often remarked that when we give a person the "right answer," we disrespect them.

Helping people develop critical thinking skills, raising their confidence level and self-esteem is actually the ultimate form of respect. It will enable your workforce to more passionately embrace improvement behaviors. Ideally, the walk should be used to develop the knowledge, skill and capability in your associates to clearly see the process involved, understand how it works and identify problems or opportunities for improvement within it.

Ask how opportunities for improvement are handled, using the walk to increase trust levels:

A. What do you typically do when a problem happens?

B. What can you do this hour/takt to remove barriers?

C. What countermeasures have you tried? What new ones will you try next?

D. How long will you test the solution (experiment) and what criteria will you use to determine if the experiment is a success?

E. If the experiment works, what changes will be necessary in order for you to sustain it?

F. Are other resources needed to help (Quality, Safety, Maintenance, Engineering, etc.)?

G. What happens if you have an idea for how to improve your work?

H. What escalation (communication) pathways exist to address unresolved issues?

When you see operating problems or opportunities, focus on one issue. Where does the problem originate? Go there. Study some more.

A. What is the team's source of information? Where is it stored? How is it developed?

B. What is being done to prevent abnormalities?

C. Do people have to guess what should be done next (e.g., which job is the next one)? Or is the "right thing" and the "right way" crystal clear even to the casual observer?

D. Is Standard Work meaningful and consistent?

E. Do people have a clear understanding of what is

expected? Has Standard Work documented those expectations?

F. How do people know they delivered what their customer required?

When you see opportunities, your job becomes to coach the team on how to capture them. Help people develop stronger critical thinking skills:

A. Is there enough detail listed for each miss?

B. Are issues listed and captured in a Pareto format for prioritization?

C. Are we attacking the top item(s)?

D. Coach the team to develop an implementation plan. Use aggressive targets on small-scoped activities.

E. Check for support systems alignment/dis-alignment to foster additional improvement (communications, planning, accountabilities, metrics, recognition, etc.).

F. Coach team members to learn how to vet improvement ideas on their own before submitting them to leadership (get agreement on shift, get agreement on other shifts, check with support personnel, and so on); this may require support systems adjustment.

G. Has the local leader assigned appropriate resources to solve problems?

H. Are coaches/resources assigned to assist problem solvers?

I. Can the problem solvers articulate the current status of their improvement activities when asked during normal reviews?

Thank and compliment the team members for sharing their thoughts. Also thank the visiting walkers.

A. If the review goes well, give positive accolades and encourage next steps.

B. If the review does not meet basic requirements, provide feedback to line leaders, CI staff, and anyone involved in coaching.

    a. Is training needed regarding how to solve problems, gather data/facts, and use appropriate tools to get to root causes?

Mark Graban shared a quote from Fujio Cho on his Lean Blog on January 20, 2011. Cho said, "We want to not only show respect to our people, in the same way, we want to show respect to everyone we meet in life, we also want to respect their humanity, what it is that makes us human, which is our ability to think and feel—we have to respect that humanity in the way we design the work, so that the work enables their very human characteristics to flourish."

DEBRIEF ACTIVITIES AFTER THE WALK

The following steps should occur after the Gemba Walk in-process/on-floor event, and are crucial demonstrations of leadership commitment.

1. How effectively was the purpose of the walk accomplished?

2. What improvement opportunities or action commitments were made during the walk?

   A. Clarify, combine and prioritize (if needed) discussion points from the Gemba Walk that need follow-up on the next walk.

   B. Document these ideas for follow-up purposes on the next walk.

   C. Decide on a timeline for implementing agreed-upon improvements. Include this review as part of follow-up activities.

   D. Note the follow-up plan to see how well improvements are implemented/sustained.

3. If a waste walk was done, get balanced inputs from the people who did the walk.

   A. Capture all opportunities identified from the whole group.

   B. Clarify follow-up commitment actions.

Troy Vellinga, former vice president of Continuous Improvement at W.W. Grainger, said, "It's important to confirm improvement actions after the walk. Capture all the improvement opportunities, then rank them to select which ones will be acted upon. At the end of many of our walks we would all work together to create a quick white board list of improvements, then we would quickly ICE (Impact, Control, Ease) rank them in an ICE matrix and pick the top one or two for action. This made sure there was action and follow-through, and something to *check* during the next walk."

It is better not to do a Gemba Walk if there is a chance that these steps will not be completed. Failure to complete them becomes evidence of a "fake" Gemba Walk that disrespects the associates involved and destroys credibility with the leadership team.

IT TAKES PRACTICE TO PERFECT THE GEMBA WALK

When you Gemba Walk, you are assessing how well your organization is attuned to seeing issues, clearing them, finding root causes and solving them. It takes practice to learn how to do this well. Elsewhere in this book we talk about Coaching Gemba Walkers. Effective coaching will move you through the learning curve more quickly.

One key point to remember: ***Don't try to do too much on a Gemba Walk!*** It is just one walk; you are unlikely to change the world with one stroll. Think of it more like a farmer planting seeds and waiting for them to grow than as a tidal wave sweeping across the operation. Have some patience. If a sufficient number of seeds get planted and they are watered and nurtured, there will be a harvest, but it will not happen overnight.

TYPICAL GEMBA WALK TYPES

Gemba Walks can take many forms, depending on the purpose, breadth of subject area view and depth of process view needed. Daniel Jones, co-author of *Lean Thinking*, had a great quote on Gemba Walks at the Association of Manufacturing Excellence (AME) Annual Conference in 2013: *"Follow an example. Follow a product all the way back from the customer right back to your raw material supplier. Follow a patient going through the hospital. Simply focus on following lots of real examples. And then ask, 'Okay, how typical is that example? How differently are other products, different patients, experiencing the system?' You start with the details and then work up from that point."*

The examples and preparation steps outlined below are intended to clear up possible confusion before the walkers hit the floor.

Later on in this book, we outline the most common types of walks and provide a few templates, which you can use as a guide in crafting a plan for your team's walk. The most common examples are summarized below:

Daily Department Gemba Walk – A walk done by the manager/supervisor/team leader and perhaps a key support person (e.g., CI manager or engineer). Daily walks in a cell have a somewhat different focus than those done by a leader from outside the area walking a larger production or operations area. Daily walks typically focus on effective "Standard Work" practices and process instability issues. Every day the leadership group is interfacing with the people who create value for the business. Note: the word "daily" does not have to mean once per day. Ideally a direct leadership team should walk key process areas multiple times a day; three is a reasonable target.

Typical Purpose – Might be any one or a combination of the following:

1. Ensure that Standard Work is being followed (validate Standard Work practices)

2. Understand progress against current target condition (performance metrics) and progress against longer-term "future state" improvement challenges

3. Look for abnormalities, and ensure they are known and a plan is in place to address them

4. Check progress since last walk, problem-solving and people development actions

5. Engage and coach associates on improvement

A stable process requires a different walk than unstable processes (see Gemba Walk Examples 1 and 2).

Weekly Leadership Team Gemba Walk – A walk done by the leadership team, with a focus on one or more cells of a larger production area, such as General Manager, Engineering, Maintenance, EH&S, etc. Done to foster cross-functional collaboration, reduction of barriers inhibiting flow, and development of critical thinking skills (by all parties). Perspective is the cell (or value adding activity) as the customer, and the leaders are the supplier to the cell.

Typical Purpose – Engage people by having them see leaders as present and connected to serving their needs. Identify coaching opportunities/needs, understand progress since last walk, observe the effectiveness of cross-functional support activities.

Value Stream Gemba Walk – Similar to the Weekly Leadership Team walk, except it covers an entire product or service value stream end-to-end. Once a cell or organization reaches this level of improvement maturity, the daily walks can begin to move their focus away from primarily looking for waste and instead look for barriers or gaps (e.g., in the Lean Flow Enterprise Elements) that inhibit the flow of value.

Typical Purpose – Discover more significant areas of waste. Learn how people currently approach improvement and coach higher-level strategic thinking on how best to eliminate waste over time. Look for improvement opportunities in the "white space" between departments since most organizations are still managed from a functional "silo" perspective.

Walk by Outside Executives – Typically a value-stream-type walk where the leaders seek to better understand the creation and flow of value across an organization. Questions from external participants are usually at a higher level (more general) than someone who is regularly walking the value stream.

Typical Purpose – Gain a deeper understanding of how people approach process improvement, their understanding of business issues, and how they think and act on improvement.

Fake Walks – Avoid doing a fake walk. Gemba Walks are ineffective when leaders do them just for show or to catch people doing something wrong and then blame them for the problem. Those types of walks convey disrespect for associates (managers and employees). Do not waste time doing a Gemba Walk unless you are committed to following through with all the steps (including any implementations and follow-up communications).

A fake walk can also happen when the area being walked is scrubbed clean or people spend extra time preparing information, data, and presentations just for the walk. This is waste! Ensure that people understand, if information is to be shared, it should be in the exact form and way they use it every day.

GEMBA WALKS IN AN OFFICE ENVIRONMENT

Doing an effective Gemba Walk in a factory environment can be a challenge, it's even more so in an office environment. Typically there is no physical product, people are multi-tasking and they are most likely not doing highly repetitive activities. In this type of an environment it's especially challenging when you first start doing them. Why?

- People being observed feel threatened by the activity. They are not used to being observed and wonder what will happen as a result (it couldn't possibly be good).

- When you do the walk, it's not always obvious what work activity will be taking place or should be taking place – given the multi-tasking activities that occur.

- Most offices do not make much use of visual reporting or standard work practices. Thus much of the work being done is hard to see.

Therefore the primary purpose of your early walks in this type of environment might be to primarily focus on building trust and making it easier to see value add and non-value adding work, using those two terms this time as activities related to the processes being observed, since most office processes do not add value in the classic sense of 'value to the customer.' The core reasons already discussed for doing Gemba Walks still apply, walkers seek to learn:

1. Learn about your current reality. What is really happening vs. your assumptions?

    a. Do people understand the work they do?

    b. What action is needed by leadership to elevate improvement maturity?

2. Develop a deeper understanding of process performance.

3. How is standard work being utilized to serve as a means to repeatable, predictable outcomes in an office environment?

4. Do clear goals exist for current short-, medium- and long-term process performance?

5. Develop people; create an environment where they can more fully use their talents, increase levels of trust and do their best work.

6. How do people approach trying to make improvement happen?

7. How actively do people surface process problems/abnormalities?

8. How robust is the support structure for local improvement activities?

The three stages of a Gemba Walk will also still apply although the perspective may differ somewhat due to the nature of the work being done. Reference the Three Stages of walk previously described. We will simply add a few additional thoughts here relative to office walks.

Define a Purpose for the Walk

You should still write down the purpose for your walk. But keep in mind that it is critical to build trust levels, especially in an environment where people are not used to being observed. Walk softly, ask questions, then – listen. Keep trying to understand what is happening from a process perspective, including who the customers are for the work activity and what impact suppliers have on the work activity.

It's often useful to follow the flow of a particular information or service process (this is particularly important in a multitasking environment). If you make certain the primary purpose of any walk is 'to learn' vs. to find something being done wrong you will be off to a good start.

Doing the Walk

Office walkers should practice "active listening" & respectfully ask probing questions based on three key activities: *Go See, Ask What Then Why, & Show Respect*.

A. *Go See* – try to learn what is happening in the current environment, you are looking for the same set of things outlined previously.

A key goal for walks in this type of environment is to make it easier to see if the right work is being done in the right way and at the right time. Multi-tasking in an office environment effectively masks key issues. And people doing the work feel this is normal, so they don't see the waste elements hidden in jumping to a new task because they cannot complete the old task. It's easy to stay busy and people are always working, but the process issues are hidden. A key part of *Go See* is trying to penetrate this fog.

In early walks you might not be able to easily see anything. As time goes by it should be easier to do this. But the goal isn't simply making stuff visible. It's more about creating a work environment where the people doing the work can see process abnormalities, make workarounds visible, and they're inspired to take action to address the issues.

Note: You can follow a process in either direction supplier-to-customer or the opposite (the latter is often more informative), also without process stability and standardization there is no basis for improvement.

B. *Ask What, Then Why* – Humble questions, seeking to understand, are the prerequisite in the Go See stage, if you wish to move on to a coaching/improvement relationship. Building on some of the questions previously suggested you might also ask:

What work activities are sitting in your queue waiting for something to happen so you can continue to work on them?

a. How is this coordinated with the suppliers or with the customers for this work from a timing perspective?

b. Are there ever issues with your inputs?

c. Do your direct customers ever have issues with your outputs?

d. How do you know when this happens?

In a factory there might be an accumulation of materials or component parts. In an office environment there might be an accumulation of work activities waiting for something to happen, before the worker's activities can resume.

Decision-making is often a key part of office processes. Standardized Work includes the way people make decisions, so during a walk one might also explore, 'when that situation arises, what do you do about it?' 'Do others handle such situations differently? Does that create any other issues?'

C. **Show Respect** – Showing respect is important for all walks. It is especially true in the initial stages of office walks. Sitting with workers in this type of an environment and actually having them talk you through the work they are doing is very helpful. For example, sitting with an order entry clerk and having them explain how they process an order, or having an accounts payable clerk show you how they process a payment request. It is always enlightening and exposes many issues that slow/disrupt or decrease the ability of the person to perform the work correctly the first time around. Most people like to talk about the work they do. Taking the time to ask them something as simple as "can you show me how you do xyz" opens the door to great learning. Seek to really understand the current state before judging, starting to coach, etc. Make sure you provide support and resources when people raise a problem.

Making office work more visual is critical

For office walks to succeed you must find ways to make important components of the work being done more visual. The visuals should provide important feedback to the people doing the work (meaning they use it to stay on pace, make problems visible, for decision making, not just rotely tracking activities) and the visuals make it easier to develop standard work routines. *Thus greatly making it easier for walkers to understand the current reality.* Here are a few examples.

Customer Service Department

Employees in this department listed all of their weekly work activities. On Monday morning all cards on the board show a Red Bar, meaning the work is not yet completed, nor is it due. Each day of the week the cards get flipped. If the task is complete, the card is turned over and a Green Bar color shows as completed. If the task is supposed to be finished, but it will probably not be completed during the day, then the card is flipped upside down and a Yellow Bar is shown. This is a signal to the rest of the team that help is needed. If the task is not completed by the end of the day the Red Bar is left showing for that particular task, then the manager knows there is an issue and can take steps to resolve the problem. The key steps for the work task are listed on one side of the card.

Employees use the cards to see who is on schedule and who has an excessive workload. Their normal condition is some days one employee will be busier than the others and one employee may have a light workday. When they look at the board it is easy to see who is running behind and who is in a position to offer to step-in and assist. This works great as work ebbs and flows between the employees. If one person consistently has problems keeping up than there is a deeper analysis to understand what is happening from a process perspective. The team felt this helped them to work more effectively together; they were the people who designed and used it.

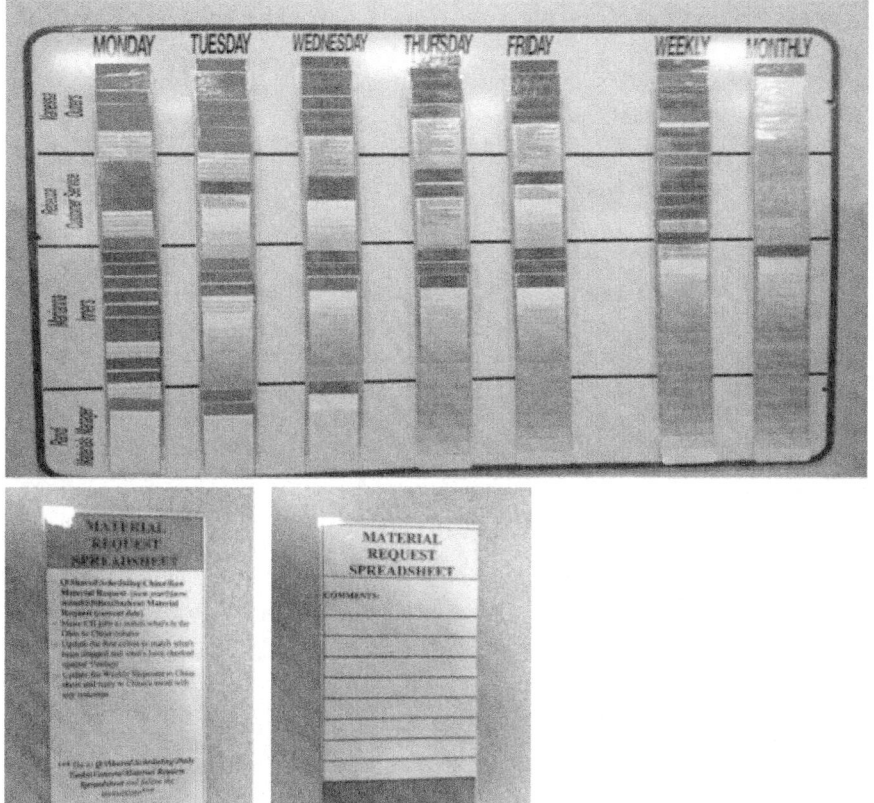

Engineering Department - Request for Proposal Process for Custom Designs

In this example the engineering department was overloaded with projects. Quite a few of the proposals were unlikely winners (the company was primarily being used for a comparative bid) and there was not much collaboration between Purchasing, Sales, and Operations. Work activities were pretty much handed off from one functional group to the next. They used this visual board to level their workloads and improve their hit rate (# of wins) on Customer Request for Proposals (RFPs). Leaders from Engineering, Purchasing, Sales, Operations review this board as part of their bi-weekly Gemba Walk standard work activities. *This picture is purposely not readable.*

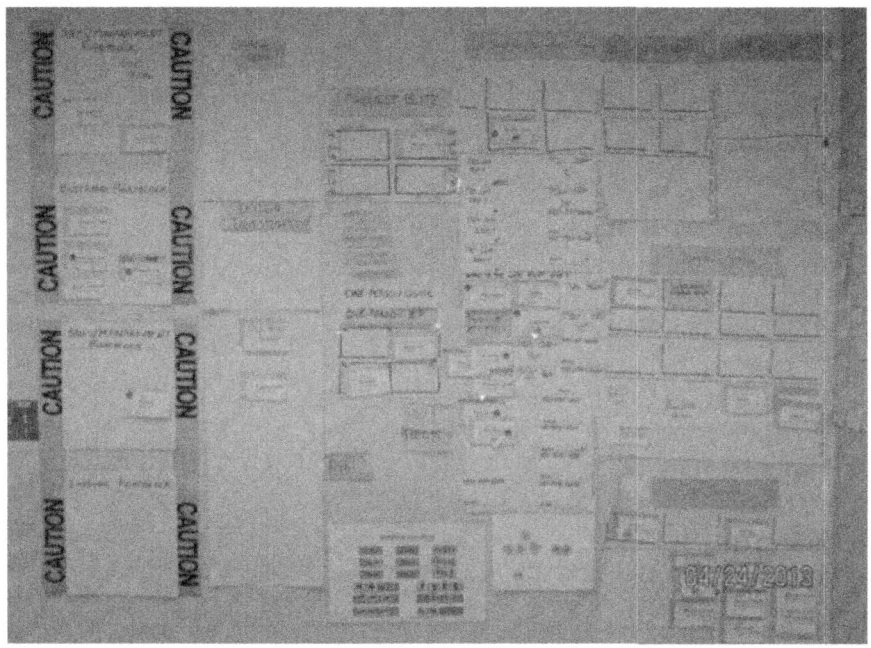

There is a lot going-on with this board. But the essence of it is simple. They realized they overloaded engineers with work, but it was not easy to see. Once this board was created a single engineer could not be working on more than four RFPs. A cross-functional group of leaders from the involved departments met twice per week to prioritize projects. The board shows the current status of the project. Once the company began to do this they increased their win rate on proposals from ~ 25% to more than 50%.

Patience

With some degree of patience, discipline and tenacity you can make progress in an office environment. Your task will be much easier (not easy) if walkers behave in the role of a servant leader who is there to see that barriers get removed. Over time credibility will be built, people in the office will develop skills and confidence and significant change can take place.

SUSTAINING THE GAINS

Sustaining the gains from improvement projects is a challenge for most organizations. It is easy to revert to the old ways of operating, especially when people are pressed for time and something needs to get done quickly. It is easy to say, "I know we came up with this new method, but just this one time, let's do it the old way, so we can get the job finished." Constant little pressures cause us to revert or to skip doing something new. Over time much of the gain slips away.

The following model highlights the elements involved in effective performance improvement. Following the ABC sequence, first we should focus on creating meaningful value for customers. Second we should align our internal processes to create value. That is not the same thing as a focus on eliminating waste. Instead, the perspective shifts to looking for barriers that inhibit value creation, which is far and away the most important waste to eliminate. The third element highlights the fact that support systems should support the organization's value creation processes.

It is very important we focus on that last dimension—*the role of support systems*. Failing to consider these frequently undermines what an organization is trying to accomplish during periods of change.

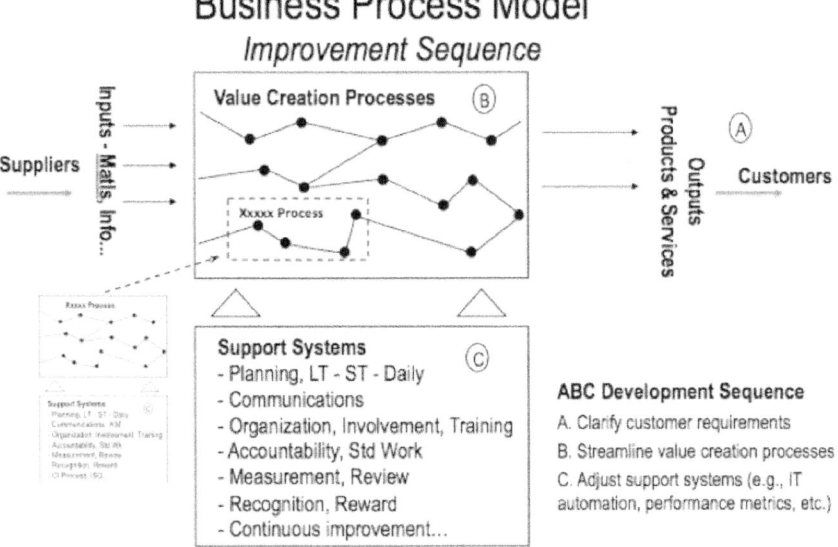

Business Process Model
Improvement Sequence

Inputs - Matls, Info...

Suppliers

Value Creation Processes (B)

Xxxxx Process

Outputs Products & Services

(A)

Customers

Support Systems (C)
- Planning, LT - ST - Daily
- Communications
- Organization, Involvement, Training
- Accountability, Std Work
- Measurement, Review
- Recognition, Reward
- Continuous improvement...

ABC Development Sequence
A. Clarify customer requirements
B. Streamline value creation processes
C. Adjust support systems (e.g., IT automation, performance metrics, etc.)

CUMBERLAND

A primary reason for this is poor management of the organization's support systems. For example:

1. Performance metrics are focused on departmental performance and do not take into account the collaboration/cooperation needed to create customer value

2. Accountabilities are fuzzy and poor performance is tolerated

3. Standard Work exists, but there are no mechanisms in place to ensure "Standard Work" is the way work should get done

4. Planning is done with little understanding or appreciation of actual process capability

5. Organizational power structures (the way the company is organized) inhibit people's ability to improve or to collaborate across departmental lines of authority, etc.

Please look at the small dashed box labeled "Xxxxxx Process" inside the Value Creation Processes box. It could be any one of the processes in a business that produces value to customers. In the sub-image shown on the lower left, notice a smaller Support Systems block under the Value Process segments block. The concept here is that every process—from enterprise to business units, to departments and work groups—has local versions of the support systems. To fully support local operations, each leader must manage her/his local support systems. Visual performance reporting at a cell or department level is one example of managing local support systems.

It's highly likely you will need to make adjustments to management support systems (communication, planning, measurement, etc.) and better align cross-functional cooperation to provide support in terms of implementing and sustaining improvements. If this is an issue in your business (and it usually is), have people from relevant support groups periodically participate in Gemba Walks. They offer a great way to see with your own eyes how effectively your support systems are operating and the positive or negative impact they have on organizational performance.

Here is a brief example of a support systems modification at Autoliv in Ogden, Utah. Employee improvement ideas used to be filtered through management, but employees were submitting so many ideas that the leadership team was becoming a bottleneck and slowing down the process.

Leadership decided to open up the process for getting improvement ideas approved. They created alternative pathways to make it easier for improvement to happen. When people had an improvement idea, they would write it down and post it on their cell information board.

Once a week in their team huddle meetings, cell members would share their improvement ideas. First of all they needed to get approval for the idea from people on their shift. Approved ideas on one shift were then shared with the other shift (via the cell leads). If the other shift approved it, team members would check with any appropriate support personnel (e.g., Engineering) and if authorized, the idea was implemented.

By making this change, Autoliv increased employee ideas from approximately 16,000 implemented in 2004 to over 100,000 implemented in 2010.

Organizational support systems definitely influence behaviors. If the support systems are not aligned to reinforce the desired new behaviors, the gains will not be sustained. And management owns the support systems.

COACHING GEMBA WALKERS

If Gemba Walks are going to become a standard new behavior for your organization, you will need ways to reinforce this new habit. Give some consideration to working with a coach. This can be someone from inside or outside the organization. You will become a much better Gemba walker with effective coaching support.

Why should someone want to be coached?

- Offers an opportunity to learn; possibly picking up something quite meaningful and useful. It can help the walker find new ways to:
  - Gain insights
  - Communicate more effectively
  - Effect change
  - Elevate average performers
- Most leaders have an intellectual understanding of lean concepts, but fewer than 5% of all leaders truly use lean concepts to transform their business or work environment

Goals of a coaching process

- A typical key objective at the start of a coaching process is *for the leader to gain more knowledge so she can ask better questions.*

- Improve leaders' (at all levels) ability to more effectively see improvement opportunities

- Accelerate rate of performance improvement

- Create an environment that raises the self-esteem, capability and confidence of the people who work for the organization

Very often an internal continuous improvement staff is given the responsibility to help create a more effective improvement culture. This may sound like a great idea, but it can be a challenge for the staff to work with successful executives. This section shares a few thoughts for internal continuous improvement practitioners to coach successful leaders.

Coaching a Successful Leader

- Get buy-in from the leader relative to the coaching process

- Consider doing (or using existing) self-assessment instruments for behavior traits the leader is trying to change

- Understand what leader seeks to accomplish from a business perspective
    - NOT selling, need to understand their needs
    - You get one chance to establish credibility

- ◦ Ask questions, do not give answers; although some sensei do the opposite

- Do an experimental walk to get an initial observation before finalizing a 'coaching agreement.'

- The focus here is on improvement effectiveness coaching, leaders may already be working with another coach on leadership skills/ behaviors...collaborate!

Once again there is a basic model for doing this effectively:

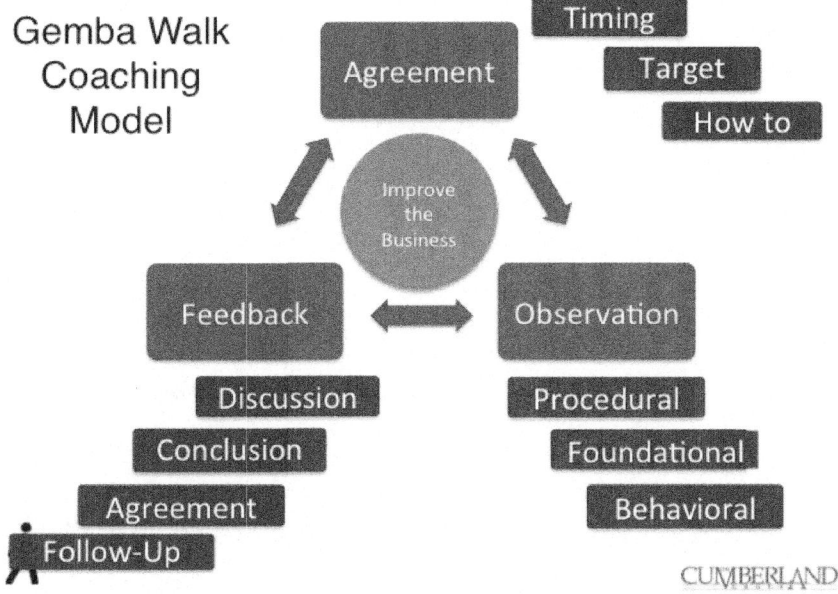

1. Create a Coaching Agreement –

Coaching successful leaders is different from coaching people that are dysfunctional. It is usually quite easy for successful leaders to help others; but may be difficult for that same person to ask for help. So start by determining the leader's level of interest and make certain there is a good fit between the leader and the coach. There may be other coaching activities already taking place inside the organization. If that is the case the CI coaches should make certain they are aligned and not competing with other coaching activities.

Develop a Blue Print for Change in terms of specific desirable behaviors

Agree on the coaching process to be used, including **confidentiality** (this is critical). Give some thought to creating a safe space (place) to give/receive feedback.

Incorporate elements related to what the leader seeks to accomplish from a business perspective or behaviors the leader seeks to change. Have the leader explain their:

1. Personal wants and needs

2. Most important values

3. Understand where the leader is trying to go

And what about other observations by the coach? Is the leader receptive to discuss them in an open-minded way? Set a time, place and frequency for the coaching sessions. Consider doing a pilot to test the agreement, making appropriate revisions after completing a couple walks.

Decide what you need to do as a coach to help the leader accomplish his/her objectives. Coaching may initially focus on making certain the leader has a deep understanding of the key foundations of world-class performance improvement practices. Most do not. Agreement considerations:

Timing

- How often will you meet?
- How long will it take?
- Where will the meeting happen?

Target – What are the leader's improvement targets relative to Gemba Walk effectiveness (this is focused on how the walk gets done)?

- Does leader understand the Gemba Walk process?
- Is the leader seeking specific feedback? If yes for what?
- If leader has other coaches, what can you reinforce?
- Select one procedural, foundational or behavior target to observe

How will the feedback be delivered and does it link to anything else?

- Preferred feedback format
- How will the coach assess the coachee's needs
- Should anyone else play a role in observing the leader's behaviors?
- How to redefine the coaching objective

2. Observe the Walker –

After an agreement is reached, then observe the walker. Does the walker move beyond the leadership basics?

Level One Leadership Basics

- Set direction with challenging targets
- Learn to more effectively see problems, abnormalities, waste, and opportunities

Level Two Leaders – Advanced

- Teach/coach associates to develop their ability to perform and to fix and improve their processes
- Have the tenacity to stay the course, yet balance that drive with a humility that permits them stay in touch with reality as it actually exists
- Align support systems (planning, measurement, communications, etc.) to elevate the organization's improvement maturity

How effectively does the walker *Go See, Ask What/Why and Show Respect*?   Do open-ended questions get asked? Does the leader really listen and avoid suggesting solutions? Does the leader take time to probe beneath the surface to gain a deeper understanding of what is being done and why it is happening? Is the leader developing similar capabilities in the people she touches? Are the walks done in a standard work type fashion?

Procedural aspects of the Gemba Walk:

- Phase 1: How well does the leader prepare for the walk?
  - Agree on purpose, scope, and behavior norms?
  - How were follow-up items from past walks handled?
  - Is there an open discussion with participants?
  - Does leader layout general plan on where to go?
  - Does the walk start and finish on time?
  - Did walkers practice one conversation at a time?

- Phase 2: How effectively does the leader do the walk?
  - What do walkers see? / What does the coach see?
  - How does the leader probe beneath the surface?
  - How does work get looked at from a process perspective?
  - How does the leader learn about organizational support systems' impact on how work gets done?
  - Does the leader develop critical thinking capabilities in other walkers & the people touched?
  - Does the walker foster support for using a

scientific approach to problem resolution and digging down to root-level causes?

Lean Foundations – Does the leader have an understanding of key foundations of lean, effective performance improvement practices?

- Concept of Gemba

- 8 Wastes

- Kaizen team and kaizen continuous improvement

- A3 or scientific problem solving

- Takt time

- Other things important to your organization

Behavioral

- How does the leader show respect?
  - Does the leader listen more than talk?

  - Does the leader come across as humble?

  - How does the leader create a safe environment for people to talk?

  - Is there a liberal use of 5 Whys to probe deeper?

  - Does the leader keep problem ownership in the right place?

  - Does the leader listen & avoid suggesting solutions?

- How do the leader's actions help people gain more confidence, skills and awareness?
- How do questions get asked?
  - Are open-ended positive questions asked? (e.g., "What are the issues that you're struggling with?" "How are you dealing with them?" vs. a more negative type question "WHY! did you put this piece of equipment here?")
  - Does the conversation focus on current state, future state and gaps?
  - How are employees being coached to develop more critical thinking skills (also walkers)?
  - How are key lean concepts being taught through the use of questions and observations?
- Phase 3: How effectively does the leader debrief and ensure self-learning after the walk?
  - What new insights were learned on the walk?
  - Do walkers understand where management support systems are dis-aligned?
  - How does the walker capture what was seen for future follow-up?
  - How well was follow-up handled from prior walk observations and discussions?
  - How do leaders replicate relevant ideas across the organization?

- ◦ Does debrief wrap-up with these questions:
  - ▪ Did we make any decisions during the walk today?
  - ▪ If yes, how are we going to communicate that decision?
  - ▪ How are we going to follow-up on progress?
- ◦ Follow-up protocols in place

3. Provide Feedback to the Leader

After the walk is finished discuss the experience and share the coaches observations. Provide the feedback in a space that is conducive to having a conversation. Make certain it is a two-way discussion. Probe further to make certain the leader understands the point you were trying to make and that your observation was indeed a correct interpretation of what was happening. Some leaders may ask for close-to-real-time feedback, make sure you have an acceptable protocol for doing this. ***Never embarrass the leader in front of another person.***

- How well does the walker feel it went?
- Discuss the leader's perspective (hopefully in a non-defensive fashion)
- Share the coach's observations
- What conclusions can be drawn?
- Is time needed for further reflection or the gathering of observations from others?

- What are the next steps?

- How will the coach follow-up?

A great coach serves as a role model for much of what we discuss in this guide and helps the leader to get into a regular habit of doing their leader standard work Gemba Walks. The coach can observe the Gemba walker's activities and suggest ways to improve the walker's effectiveness. Leaders should ensure their coach is a good one. With an effective coach, three things should happen relatively quickly. You should:

1. Gain new insights, causing you to change your perspective somewhat.

2. Communicate more effectively with your subordinates and your peers. This typically means you listen more than you talk.

3. See some progress in a relatively short period of time. There should be more wins than losses as a result of the steps you take to change. This is an experiment. You are learning, yet it is important to remember you will *not* get everything right the first time you try it.

If those three things are not happening, get a new coach.

Self-Assessment without a formal coach

If you find your walks are not yielding the insights or impact you hoped for, the following outline describes a few thoughts for your consideration.

One key point to remember, mentioned earlier but worth repeating: Don't try to do too much on a Gemba Walk! It is just one walk; you are unlikely to change the world with one stroll. Periodically take time to assess what you are trying to accomplish by doing these walks. A great time for a reflective dialogue on Gemba Walks is to do this as part of your debriefing activities. Have people write down the actual questions asked during the walk. During your reflection period, discuss the following:

1. Do the questions asked build the self-esteem of your associates (are they non-judgmental)?

2. What was done well during this walk?

3. What could be done better during the next walk? Prioritize and select one or two items from this list to practice on your next walk.
   A. Are open or closed questions asked?
   B. How much listening was done vs. leaders talking?
   C. What is not happening that you expected to occur? Write it down.

4. Does the questioner remain humble (a spirit of learning), or does he or she jump to problem-solving diagnosis too quickly?

5. Can you define a way to measure progress closing the gap from the current reality to the desired target condition?

If you do not have a coach give some consideration to assigning someone the responsibility to observe desired/ undesired behaviors and provide feedback after the next walk (this might be done with the group overall or one-on-one as appropriate – don't embarrass anyone, including yourself).

Other than a first line supervisors daily walks it's good to plan doing the work with several people if for no other reason than *it's tougher to put it off if someone is scheduled to go with you.*

Approach this entire process as an experiment, a learning opportunity. It might take several years to become comfortable and highly effective at doing this. That is okay.

GEMBA ASSESSMENT SYSTEM AT OC TANNER

OC Tanner, a company based in Salt Lake City, offers some useful examples of actions you can take from an organizational perspective to help people develop more effective behaviors. OC Tanner develops employee recognition strategies and rewards programs that help companies appreciate people who do great work. They have been on a lean performance improvement journey for more than 15 years and have created an assessment process to help reinforce Standard Work and coaching practices.

OC Tanner wanted to combine a number of audits they were doing into one process. All leaders at the company have coaching responsibilities and they are expected to go to Gemba to ensure Standard Work practices are working effectively. They still do Gemba Walks, in addition to weekly assessment activities outlined below.

Their Gemba Assessment System is designed to accomplish several goals:

1. Provide a means for management and teams to understand how well the supply chain is living and sustain the principles and practices necessary for success,

including: safety, lean, coaching, ISO, standardized work, security and quality.

2. Help teams understand expectations and the importance of meeting them.

3. Use the results of assessments to focus on areas that need improvement.

4. Engage all levels of management in positive interactions with teams and team members on at least a weekly basis.

How it works

Gemba assessment cards have been created for all areas of the supply chain and cover the critical systems that must be monitored, sustained and continuously improved. Each week all members of leadership from vice presidents to facilitators (their term for supervisors) select a card. The card tells the assessor which team to go to and what they need to look for. They are designed to take approximately 5 – 10 minutes to complete.
The assessor should:

1. Notify the area lead before starting the assessment.

2. Let the team member doing the work know the outcome of the assessment in a positive, helpful manner.

3. Mark the assessment card as "pass" or "no pass," inserting an "X" beside any item that did not pass – then write the date and their name on the card.

4. Fill out the assessment log, leaving the "countermeasure" and "completion date" fields blank for the team to complete.

5. Put the card on the team's metric board (card holder), green side up if passed, red side up if not passed.

Example of Gemba Standard Work Assessment Card (front side)

Std Work Lacquer/Polymer Cruisers Rev.11/15/13	
Mark non-conformities with an 'X'. 1 or more 'X' equals a 'No Pass'	
Invite the facilitator to join you for this gemba	
	Only 1 emblem on the screen.
	Spray, turn, spray again in same direction. Repeat if needed.
Why? For even coverage.	
	Did the operator verify that coverage is even and complete?
	Emblem stays on drying station until light flashes.
Why? To ensure the lacquer/polymer is dry for polishing.	
Assessment Status	
Pass	No Pass
Date:	
Assessor:	

Example of Coaching Audit Card (front side)

Coaching Huddles Jade	
Mark non-conformities with an 'X'. 1 or more 'X' equals a 'No Pass'	
Ask 2 team members:	
	Is the huddle opening engaging and fun?
	Is the huddle closing engaging and high energy?
	Does the huddle last no more than 15 minutes?
	How does the huddle connect you to each other and the day's work?
	Does the huddle include appreciation?
	Does team talk about previous day's performance and solutions to problems?
	How are goals for the day set?
	In the huddle, what opportunities do you have to learn and grow?
Assessment Status	
Pass	No Pass
Date:	
Assessor:	

Jade is one of the production teams inside OC Tanner. Coaching record includes managers meeting with people being coached. Records are up to date. Multiple types of 'audit' cards exist for this cell: visual board status, improvement activities, team huddles (shown above), equipment calibration, etc. A card is selected at random by the reviewer. An audit can be completed in less than 15 minutes.

Example of Gemba Assessment Card (back side)

The green side of the card is inserted into the cardholder on the metric board for that work area if the audit passed. If the audit was "no pass," the red side is shown sticking out of the card pocket.

The cell teams are responsible for responding to the assessment. They take the following steps:

1. Create a red/green improvement opportunity card for each failed assessment and discuss how to improve the task (a copy of this is not included here, it's their write-up card on actions the cell plans to take to address issues from the audit).

2. Discuss results of the audits in daily support team huddles, celebrating successful assessments and getting help as needed to resolve red/green card issues.

3. Managers (the next level up) or facilitators (supervisors) also discuss the results of Gemba Assessments in their team huddle meetings and the resources needed to resolve red/green card issues.

If the cell did not pass its audit, they need to provide an update at the next tier manager's huddle regarding what actions (countermeasures) are being taken to address the shortfall.

GEMBA GONE WRONG!

A story shared by a former Toyota manager described one of his learning experiences about how to do the walk. *"I recall another of my valuable lessons from my Japanese trainer concerning the Gemba. It occurred early in my career just after being promoted to Plant Manager of Assembly at Toyota's Kentucky facility. We were experiencing our first major model change. This is the 'big' change that happens every five years in the auto industry where basically the entire car changes. The years in between are minor changes. It was our first as a plant, which meant that there were new parts from new suppliers, new equipment, and new standardized work for all the team members.*

"Needless to say, we were experiencing many problems. My trainer told me to make sure I spent time at the Gemba during this time of many problems. At Toyota, problems are identified with an Andon pull, which stops the line to maintain quality; but then our productivity suffers. At the end of the line, if a car had a defect that couldn't be repaired with an Andon pull, it had to go to an 'off-line repair area.' The Toyota trainers set up standards for these repair areas and if, for example, the assembly repair area hit its maximum, then I was to stop the whole line. And that's exactly what was happening, so that is where I was spending my time. I was

running from the repair areas back to the end of the line, trying to identify cars that needed off-line repairs and calling over group leaders (supervisors) to try to fix them before they had to go off-line. This would 'save a car' from going off-line and maintain the quality and hopefully get our productivity back up. We were working very hard!

"It wasn't long before my trainer arrived and asked, 'What are you doing?' I was proud of how hard I was working at the Gemba 'in the heat of the battle' and explained to him my goal of maintaining quality and raising productivity. He asked many questions and then walked me back along the assembly line observing the 500 team members working their processes. There he asked me more questions, the ones I remember being, 'What do you see and hear?' There were dozens of Andons being pulled, lighting the lights and sounding the musical alarms. There were team leaders rushing to help many frustrated team members.

*"Through his coaching, questions and guidance he helped me to understand I was at the Gemba, but I was in the wrong place doing the wrong thing. I was managing results and putting Band-Aids on problems. **I needed to be managing the process, helping my group leaders, team leaders and team members to solve their problems.** A valuable lesson in my lean journey."*

The trainer's questions helped the young manager radically alter his perspective and improved his ability to more effectively define his standard work actions moving forward.

GEMBA WALK EXAMPLE GUIDES

Several example outlines for doing a Gemba Walk are offered below. They may serve as useful templates for Gemba Walks you plan to do:

The following diagram might be helpful as you create your own Gemba Walks for specific purposes. Like the simple "Go see, ask why, show respect," the diagram indicates appropriate behaviors that, when applied to various steps in a Gemba Walk, make it respectful, empowering and effective.

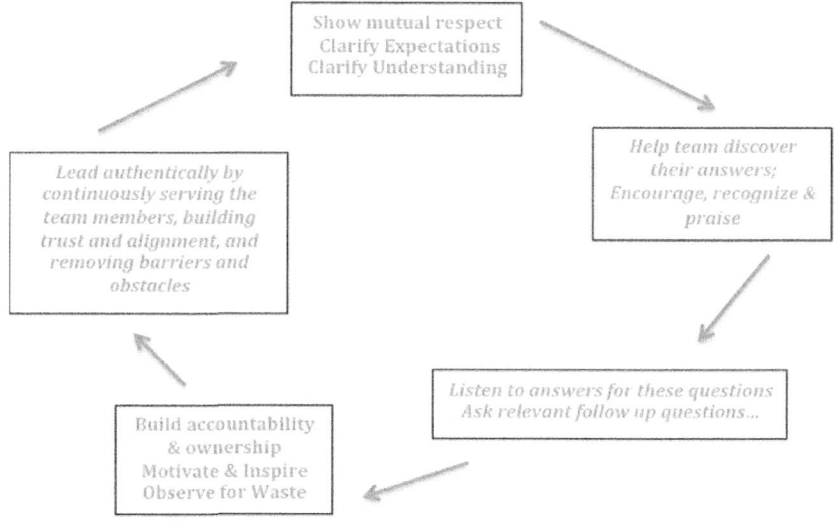

The examples are not intended as a script. Look at the various perspectives for doing a Gemba Walk and determine if any apply to the walk you plan to do. If yes, use the example as a template for creating your walk plan.

Example 1: Daily Gemba Walk Outline (Stable Process)
Example 2: Daily Gemba Walk Outline (Unstable Process)
Example 3: Value Stream or Waste Walk Outline

EXAMPLE 1: DAILY GEMBA WALK OUTLINE – STABLE PROCESS

A process is **stable** when it regularly meets takt times or performance targets.

Determine the Purpose for your walk (write it down), recognizing that you would typically seek to achieve the following:

1. Determine if processes are in alignment with what organization seeks to accomplish

2. Check on progress since last walk, problem-solving & people development actions

3. Identify opportunities to improve upon current standard (if everything is green, that is a problem)

4. Engage and coach line leaders and associates to elevate improvement maturity

Go See (use the walk to learn what is actually happening on a regular basis):

1. Start at the metrics board and check current status (this hour) of Standard Work/takt progress. Ask the team:

A. Did we make takt or target last hour?

B. Are we going to make it this hour/takt?

C. If the answer is no to either question, ask why not.

2. Observe the process:

A. Look at Standard Work documents to understand flow opportunities

B. Look at gaps in cycle times (cycle time repeatability/reliability)

C. Look at quality at the source and at quality outcomes

D. Look at upstream (supplier) and downstream (customer) interface connections

E. Look at workplace organization and visual systems

F. Look for improvement opportunities and waste

Ask What, Then Why (learn what is happening so you can more effectively lead improvement endeavors, keeping in mind the way you ask questions, your body language and inquiry vs. judgment will foster how open people are willing to be with you):Your first question should be a "What?" Follow that up with "Whys?" to better understand.

1. What is the primary purpose of this work activity?

A. What are you trying to accomplish?

B. Who is the customer for this work activity?

C. Why is this your target?

2. As you make the above observations, look for inconsistencies and awkwardness or things that are difficult to do. Then ask questions such as:

   A. Why does the work need to be done this way?

   B. Why has this issue not been addressed?

   C. What ideas do you have to improve the process?

   D. What improvement activities are underway in this process?

Show Respect (use the walk to increase trust levels by asking): What help do you need from me or anyone else?

1. Can other areas benefit from your improvement? Have you shared it?

2. Ask open-ended questions to better understand team members' thought processes.

3. Help the team prioritize opportunities.

4. Congratulate leaders & team members on takt or target accomplishment.

5. Learn how team attained takt time or target results (how they achieved stability).

Coach Effective Problem Solving (help people develop stronger critical thinking skills by asking):

1. Since the process is relatively stable, what is being done to take it to the next level of performance (target condition)?

2. Is key process waste identified?

3. Is the team seeking to eliminate meaningful barriers to creating customer value ?

4. Check support systems alignment/dis-alignment to foster additional improvement (communications, planning, accountabilities, metrics, recognition, etc.).

5. Coach team members on how to vet improvement ideas on their own before submitting to leadership (get agreement on shift, on other shifts, check with support personnel, and so on); this may require support systems adjustment.

6. Are issues listed and captured in a Pareto format for prioritization?

7. Are we attacking the top item(s)?

8. Have local leaders assigned appropriate resources to solve problems?

9. Are coaches/resources assigned to assist problem solvers?

10. Can the problem solvers articulate the current status of their improvement activities when asked during normal reviews?

11. If the review goes well, give positive accolades and encourage next steps.

12. If the review does not meet basic requirements, provide feedback to line leaders, CI staff, and anyone involved in coaching. Is training needed regarding how to solve problems, gather data/facts, and use appropriate tools to get to root causes?

Using a Coaching Kata or Improvement Kata Approach
(When talking with the person being coached, ask):

1. What is the target condition you are trying to reach (Understand the direction)?

2. What is the actual current condition (Grasp the current condition)?

   A. What was your last step?

   B. What did you expect (to happen)?

   C. What actually happened?

   D. What did you learn?

3. What obstacles do you think are preventing you from reaching the target condition?

4. What is your next step (Plan/Do/Check/Act—problem-solving experiment)? What do you expect to see as a result of that experiment?

5. How can we Go See what we have learned from taking that step (this becomes a Gemba Walk point of focus)?

6. Once the target condition is realized and stable, establish the next target condition.

When the walk is done:

1. What steps can you take to create a more effective environment where people can do their best work?

2. What insights did you gain?

3. What items/actions need follow-up on the next walk through this area?

EXAMPLE 2: DAILY GEMBA WALK OUTLINE – UNSTABLE PROCESS

A process is **unstable** when Standard Work is not defined or there is wide variation taking place in the process (or takt is frequently not being met).

Determine the Purpose for your walk (write it down), recognizing that you would typically seek to achieve the following:

1. Understand why Standard Work is not driving takt or target performance attainment

2. Attack Abnormalities that cause people to miss takt/targets

3. Instill a sense of urgency and capability in the team to win every hour

Go See (use the walk to learn what is actually happening on a regular basis):

1. Start at the metrics board and check current status (this hour) of Standard Work/takt progress. Ask the team:

1. What is the target? Why is that the target?

2. Did we make takt or target last hour? If not, why not?

3. Are we going to make it this hour/takt? If not, why not?

2. Observe the process:

   1. Is the line/cell/group staffed with trained members per Standard Work?

   2. Does the WIP amount equal the standard?

   3. Is there material available for the team to obtain this takt or hour?

   4. Is the material available for the next takt or hours, per plan?

   5. Are operators capable of reaching planned cycle time per Standard Work?

   6. Does the equipment enable stability? How can you judge?

Ask What, Then Why (learn what is happening so you can more effectively lead improvement endeavors, keeping in mind that the way you ask questions, your body language and inquiry vs. judgment will foster how open people are willing to be):

1. Your first question should be a "What?"

   1. What is the primary purpose of this work activity?

   2. What are you trying to accomplish?

3. Who is the customer for this work activity?

2. As you make the above observations, look for inconsistencies, awkwardness or things that are difficult to do. Then begin asking "why"-type questions (probe to learn more):

   A. Why is the line over/under-staffed?

   B. Why is the WIP out of standard?

   C. Why is there no material or too much material?

   D. Why is actual/planned cycle time > takt time?

   E. Why does work get done this way?

   F. Why has this issue not been addressed?

Show Respect (use the walk to increase trust levels). Ask:

1. What do you typically do when a problem happens?

2. What can *you* do this hour/takt to remove barriers?

3. What countermeasures have you tried?

4. What new ones will we try next?

5. How long will you test the solution (experiment)?

6. What criteria will you use to determine if the experiment is a success?

7. If the experiment works, what changes will be necessary in order to sustain it?

8. Are other resources needed to help (Quality, Safety, Maintenance, Engineering, etc.)?

9. Do you feel there is a clear communication path for escalation of unresolved issues?

Coach Effective Problem Solving (help people develop stronger critical thinking skills):

1. Is there enough detail listed for each miss?

2. Are issues listed and captured in a Pareto format for prioritization?

3. Are we attacking the top item(s)?

4. Coach the team to develop an implementation plan. Use aggressive targets on small-scoped activity.

5. Check for support systems alignment/dis-alignment to foster additional improvement (communications, planning, accountabilities, metrics, recognition, etc.).

6. Coach team members to learn how to vet improvement ideas on their own before submitting them to leadership (get agreement on shift, get agreement on other shifts, check with support personnel, and so on); this may require support systems adjustment.

7. Has the local leader assigned appropriate resources to solve problems?

8. Are coaches/resources assigned to assist problem solvers?

9. Can the problem solvers articulate the current status of their improvement activities when asked during normal reviews?

10. If the review goes well, give positive accolades and encourage next steps.

11. If the review does not meet basic requirements, provide feedback to line leaders, CI staff, and anyone involved in coaching vs. training needed regarding how to solve problems, gather data/facts, and use appropriate tools to get to root causes.

Using a Coaching Kata or Improvement Kata Approach (When talking with the person being coached, ask):

1. What is the target condition you are trying to reach (Understand the direction)?

2. What is the actual current condition (Grasp the current condition)?

   A. What was your last step?

   B. What did you expect (to happen)?

   C. What actually happened?

   D. What did you learn?

3. What obstacles do you think are preventing you from reaching the target condition?

4. What is your next step (Plan/Do/Check/Act—problem-solving experiment)? What do you expect to see as a result of that experiment?

5. How can we Go See what we have learned from taking that step (this becomes a Gemba Walk point of focus)?

6. Once the target condition is realized and stable, establish the next target condition.

When the walk is done:

1. What steps can you take to create a more effective environment where people can do their best work?

2. What insights did you gain?

3. What items/actions need follow-up on the next walk through this area?

EXAMPLE 3: VALUE STREAM OR WASTE WALK OUTLINE

If the processes are not stabilized and making effective use of Standard Work, this makes walking the value stream more challenging because too much variation exists. However, that is a normal condition early in an organization's improvement journey. A key purpose of this kind of walk is to help stabilize process performance.

Determine the Purpose for your walk (write it down), recognizing that you would typically seek to support:

1. Aligning processes with what the organization is trying to accomplish.

2. Doing the walk to get a better understanding of reality, learn how effectively the organization improves, and role model effective improvement behaviors.

3. Helping leaders, managers and team members more clearly see the process, understand how it works, and identify problems or opportunities in it.

4. Gaining deeper understanding of cross-functional collaboration and timeliness.

Go See (use the walk to learn what is actually happening on a regular basis):

1. Follow the flow to understand the process (if a value stream map is available, walk the map).

    A. Pretend you are a piece of work and follow the process backwards from end to beginning.

    B. Note where and how many times work waits for transportation or processing.

    C. Note what signals get sent upstream to pull work to the next operation.

    D. Note how operators perceive upstream and downstream colleagues.

    E. Look at the tools, fixtures and storage devices used at each operation.

    F. Do the metrics boards in use foster collaboration and improvement activities throughout the value stream?

    G. Is the material available for the next takt or hours, per plan?

    H. Are operators capable of reaching planned cycle time per Standard Work?

    I. Does the equipment enable stability? How can you judge?

    J. Do workers encounter stress or strain when performing their work cycle?

2. A waste walk involves a similar questioning approach, but use the Classic Waste Checklist as a guide.

Ask What, Then Why (learn what is happening so you can more effectively lead improvement endeavors.; the way you ask questions, keeping in mind that your body language and inquiry vs. judgment will foster how open people are willing to be with you):

1. At each step along the way the first question should be a 'What?'

   A. What is the primary purpose of this work activity?

   B. What are you trying to accomplish?

   C. What is the signal telling you work needs to be done?

   D. Who is the customer for your work and how do you know if you fully met their needs?

   E. How do your suppliers (internal) know if they met your requirements?

   F. What is the condition of your equipment and do you experience unplanned downtime?

   G. How do you measure a successful workday?

   H. What are typical problems or interruptions that occur in a workday? What happens when that occurs?

   I. What happens if you have an idea for how to improve it?

2. Where there are issues with the above observations (questions), ask probing questions about 'why?'

   A. Why is this the right way to do the work?

   B. Why were the parts not available?

   C. Why are you waiting for work?

   D. Why was it difficult to know what to do next?

   E. Why is it difficult to do the right thing?

3. Remember, as a leader, it is not your job to identify or fix the problem. If you take responsibility for the fix, you will have a lot of extra work to do. Ideally you are developing these skills in your subordinates. You may need to make adjustments to the management systems (communication, planning, measurement, etc.) or align other cross-functional groups to provide support in terms of getting improvements implemented.

Show Respect (use the walk to increase trust levels). Ask:

1. What help do you need from me or anyone else?

2. Can other areas benefit from your improvement? Have you shared it?

3. Ask open-ended questions to help better understand the team members' thought processes.

4. Help the team prioritize opportunities.

5. Learn how the team attained takt time or target results (how stability was achieved).

6. Congratulate the line leader and team members on takt or target accomplishments.

Coach Effective Problem Solving (help people develop stronger critical thinking skills):

1. Coach the team to develop an implementation plan. Use aggressive targets on small-scoped activity.

2. Align support systems to foster additional improvement (communications, planning, accountabilities, metrics, recognition, etc.).

3. Coach team members to learn how to vet improvement ideas on their own before submitting them to leadership (get agreement on shift, get agreement on other shifts, check with support personnel, and so on); this may require support systems adjustment.

When the walk is done:

1. Is the current condition stable or unstable in terms of process reliability?

2. Do performance metrics in use foster collaboration between people, teams and departments?

3. What steps can you take to create a more effective environment where people can do their best work?

4. What insights did you gain?

5. What items/actions need follow-up on the next walk through this area?

CLASSIC WASTE CHECKLIST

Waste is found in all business processes. It adds no value to products and services, and it inhibits an organization's ability to create value for customers. Use the waste checklist below as a periodic reference to enhance a Gemba Walk.

1. **Inventory**: In excess of immediate needs; work-in-process queues, material stock rooms, document files, in-baskets, etc.

2. **Over-Production**: Beyond what is really needed to meet the customer requirements (e.g., 10 units vs. 8 ordered), or scrap (which is wasted production). Over-production is not just a problem in manufacturing. In software development, excess computer code is an example.

3. **Over-Processing**: Work beyond what is needed to prevent errors, defects, etc. (e.g., a one-time spreadsheet that became routine; surface finish above real requirements). Rework to correct defects in documents or materials from processing, handling, etc. is actually a form of over-processing. Extra "test" in a hospital is another example of this waste.

4. **Defects/Errors**: Resulting from uncorrectable production problems, information flaws, component defects, or...

5. **Transportation**: Movement of documents or materials adds no value to delivered information or products (however, some services may require transportation).

6. **Motion of Personnel**: Walking around looking for something, or delivering to the next step in the sequence—especially if this involves longer distances or is done more often than necessary to produce the desired results.

7. **Time Spent Waiting**: For example...

   A. Delays and waiting between uncoordinated processes

   B. Searching for information, files, IT screens, parts, and tools not right "at hand"

   C. Rethinking; like re-planning non-standard work, on the fly

8. **Lost Human Talent**: Especially untapped personnel ideas and efforts for continuous improvement of business operations; capabilities/talents repressed or not fully developed.

LEAN FLOW ENTERPRISE ELEMENTS

In addition to the Classic Waste Checklist above, a Gemba Walk might focus on one or more of the Lean Flow Enterprise Elements as listed in the themed groups below.

These are Lean Flow operating characteristics. When in place, they will be visible either in physical work areas, as operating documents or on-line, or in interpersonal working relationships. They are all important for a holistic approach to effective lean practices. Gemba Walks are easiest for those Lean Flow Elements that lend themselves to physical observations.

More detailed explanations of the items listed below are available upon request.

Theme 1—Overall Enterprise Characteristics

1. Customer/supplier partnership, satisfaction and loyalty

2. Clear output requirements

3. High-quality products and services

4. Strategic position in the industry

5. Evolving lean products, services (lean product, service and process design)

6. Production flexibility

7. Minimum-cost production

8. Minimal WIP and FG inventories

Theme 2—Workload Leveling

1. Smoothed production. Schedule linearity. Operate using takt time as a pacemaker across the organization

2. Balanced workloads and crew assignment

3. Team-based dynamic load sharing

4. Communications, visual signals

Theme 3—Efficient Workplace

1. One-piece flow throughout the operation

2. "Pull" methods, Kanbans

3. Organized "5S" workplace

4. Quick tools and fixtures

5. Quick setups and change-overs

6. Communications, visual signals

Theme 4—Dependable Processes and Equipment

1. Standardized work practice (leaders and team members)

2. Effective customer/supplier hand-offs

3. Error-proofing, prevention, poke yoke, SPC

4. Total Productive Maintenance (TPM)

5. Communications, visual signals

Theme 5—Efficient Layout

1. All process steps "in line"
2. Minimum moves, handling and transportation
3. Process synchronization
4. "Autonomation," Jidoka
5. Communications, visual signals

Theme 6—Support Systems Practices

1. Standard Work methods
2. Organization, involvement and accountability
3. Planning; LT, ST, real-time
4. Continuous flow
5. Alignment of daily activities with business strategy
6. Clear accountabilities
7. Communications, visual signals
8. Measurement and review
9. Recognition and reward
10. Continuous Improvement (CI), Kaizen
11. Leadership practices for lean Sigma CI
12. IT systems performance
13. IT systems developments
14. Problem escalation system

Paragraph descriptions of each item above are available in our Lean Flow Enterprise Elements (separate document, available upon request).

THANKS

Thank you for reading our book. It became a recipient of a Shingo Research and Professional Publication award in 2016. If you enjoyed it and feel it is worthwhile for other people to read, ***please post a review on the site where you purchased it.*** You might also send us an e-mail and we will put your comments on our website. Michael@cumberlandchicago.com

We are interested in your feedback. Please feel free to share your thoughts on how we might improve this guide and let us know what you found most helpful. We will periodically update the material.

You are welcome to connect with me on LinkedIn or Twitter: **Michael Bremer** at LinkedIn or @michaelbremer for Twitter

ABOUT THE AUTHOR

Background

Executive Director, Chicagoland Lean Enterprise Consortium
President, The Cumberland Group – Chicago
Executive Education Faculty – University of Chicago Graham
School
Vice President, AME Manufacturing Excellence Awards
(volunteer)

Michael Bremer is a nationally recognized speaker on
process improvement, lean manufacturing, leadership, and
management team effectiveness. He has thirty years'

experience, including as director of the information systems group for a Fortune 25 company, chief financial officer for an international association and president of several new business start-ups. He created a global-based continuous improvement process for a conglomerate that owned more than 400 separate profit centers, and his model was among those used to establish criteria for the Malcolm Baldrige Quality Award.

Michael is an executive with broad domestic and international industry experience in business process improvement, Toyota Production System (Lean) methods, Six Sigma, post-ERP business process performance improvement (financial and operational), project team development, lean accounting and continuous improvement. He initially studied quality improvement with Dr. Deming and Dr. Juran in the early 1980s. He has worked in a variety of environments: high and low tech manufacturing, electric utilities, USAF, USN, software, newspaper publishing, and Fortune 500 companies, including Robert Woods Johnson Foundation, Bristol-Myers-Squib, Apple Computer, General Atomics and Hallmark.

He is president of The Cumberland Group, executive director of the Chicagoland Lean Enterprise Consortium (leverage learning network) and an adjunct faculty member at the University of Chicago's Graham School. Michael has been a speaker for the American Quality & Productivity Center and the Association of Manufacturing Excellence, and also spoke at the White House Conference on Productivity. He serves on the national board of the Association of Manufacturing Excellence, and is a past board member of the Strategic Management Association and past board president of Old Town School of Folk Music.

Michael has a Bachelor of Science degree in business from the University of Missouri – St. Louis and is a Six Sigma Black Belt, CPA, and CMC. He has published a number of articles on process improvement, corporate strategy and performance metrics. He co-authored *Escape the Improvement Trap*, published by CRC Press (2010), and the *Six Sigma Black Belt Handbook*, and was lead author for *Six Sigma Financial Tracking & Reporting*, both published by McGraw-Hill.

ABBREVIATED TERMS

CI = Continuous Improvement

LT = Long Term

ST = Short Term

P/D/C/A = Plan, Do, Check, Act (aka: Plan/Do/Study/Adjust) problem-solving methodology

SME = Subject matter expert

FURTHER READING REFERENCES

1. Steven Spear, *High Velocity Edge*. McGraw-Hill, 2008

2. Mike Rother, *Toyota Kata*. McGraw-Hill. 2010

3. Michael Bremer and Brian McKibben, *Escape the Improvement Trap*. Productivity Press, 2010

4. Michael Bremer, Tom McCarty, Loraine Daniels, Praveen Gupta, *Six Sigma Black Belt Handbook*. McGraw Hill, 2004

5. Jim Womack, *Gemba Walks*. Lean Enterprise Institute, 2011

THANKS TO OUR REVIEWERS

We have interacted with a great number of people and organizations over the last 30 years and learned much from those experiences. We also had some fantastic support from people who reviewed several drafts of this e-book. We would like to recognize them for the many insights, stories and support they shared.

Cheryl Asper – Executive Assistant at OC Tanner
Michel Baudin – Owner, Takt Times Group
Kyle Edwards – President, Triton Manufacturing
Tom Hartman – Director of Operations, Autoliv Americas
Mike Hoseus – Executive Director, CQPQ and former Assistant General Manager of Manufacturing and Human Resources, Toyota Motor Manufacturing and Engineering, North America
George Koenigsaecker – former President, Jacobs Vehicle Equipment Co., author, investor
Frank Koentgen – CEO at Ozgene
Jeffrey Liker – Professor, University of Michigan, author and long-time student of Toyota
Dan McDonnell – Vice President, Operational Excellence, Ingersoll Rand

Jack McQuellon – Retired executive, Caterpillar, Inc.

Brian McKibben – Senior Vice President, The Cumberland Group

Gary Peterson – Executive Vice President, Supply Chain & Production, OC Tanner

Mark Preston – President, Riverwood Assoc.

Mike Toussaint – Manager of Strategic Initiatives at Kaman Precision Products

Mike Rother – Engineer, independent researcher, teacher, author on Toyota practices

Tom Sheffrey – Independent consultant, Anchorage, AK

Ellen Sieminski – Lean Leader at Littelfuse

Pat Wardwell – Chief Operating Officer at GBMP

Troy Vellinga – Continuous Improvement Lead at W.W. Grainger

Printed in Great Britain
by Amazon

19458475R00078